CAGE CULTURE IN OPEN WATER

TOWARDS THE BLUE REVULUTION

Amol U Khillare

2020

CAGE CULTURE
IN
OPEN WATER

Towards the Blue Revolution

AUTHOR

AMOL U KHOLLARE

CONTACTS

❖ **Address**

Residential address: At. Post. Yeldari (camp), Tq. Jintur, Dist. Parbhani-431510

Plant address: Yeldari Dam, Tq. Jintur, Dist. Parbhani.

❖ **Mobile number** : **+91-9421630706 (Whatsapp)** **+91-8805976706**

❖ **E-mail** : lumbiniaqua007@gmail.com amolkhillare007@gmail.com

AUTHOR'S PROFILE

Mr. Amol Uddhav Khillare is mechanical engineering by profession and his family business is traditional fishing. After completion of course  he proposes to setup a fish culture unit and food processing rather than going for employment. He has gained vast experience in fish farming in business line of Indian major carp. He also achieves field knowledge as well as experience activity. He has very well known about the proposed activity deeply and also knows about market for raw material as well as the market selling the products. His family has 30 years experience in traditional fishing. He got national and states training from state government and central government. He got training organised by National Fisheries development Board (NFDB) Hyderabad in CIFRI Kolkata West Bengal, KVK Raipur Chhattisgarh and Central Institute of Fishery Education (CIFE) Mumbai. And now they are educating fish farmers and providing services to them related fish farming and marketing. He wants to maximise fish production in India and doing hard work for providing fresh and hygienic fish for our country. They are well known if fisherman and fish farmer are made aware, fish production can definitely increase.

Adv. Gautam G Khade

Services and Suppliers

Lumbini Aquaculture

1. Best Cage Culture Installation
2. Best Fish Feed
3. Detailed Project Reports (DPR) and Statistics
4. Best Fish Seed
5. Ornamental Fishes with Fish Tank.
6. Boats with Engine
7. Medicine
8. Pond Constriction Help
9. Water Quality Management
10. Fish market availability
11. Transportation
12. Cold Storage
13. Mentoring
14. Training
15. Machines and instrument

Index

Sr.no.	Title	Page no.
1.	INTRODUCTION	6
2.	INDIAN FISHERY - AN OVERVIEW	8
3.	WHAT IS CAGE CULTURE?	11
4.	ADVANTAGES AND DISADVANTAGES OF CAGE CULTURE	12
5.	DESIGN AND CONSTRUCTION	14
6.	INVIRONMENTAL IMPACT OF CAGE CULTURE	15
7.	STEPS OF CAGE CULTURE	16
8.	PROCUREMENT OF CAGE MATERIALS	17
9.	INSTALLIONS OF CAGES	19
10.	SELLECTION OF STOCKING MATERIALS	20
11.	PANGASIUS	21
12.	CAGE AND STOCK MAINTAINCE	22
13.	SUPPLIMENTARY FEEDING	24
14.	MARKET ANALYSIS	26
15.	DEMAND	27

INTRODUCTION

Cage is an enclosed space of rear organism in water that maintain free exchange of water with the surrounding water body, cage culture is an aquaculture production system where fish are held in floating net pens. Cage culture of fish utilizes existing water resources but encloses the fish in a cage or basket which allows water to pass freely between the fish and the pond permitting water exchange and waste removal into the surrounding water. India is having big potential of Cage Culture, because lake is having deep and sufficient water availability. This project will help to empowerment fisherman and ruler entrepreneurship development. This project is also helpful for employment generation program, it providing many people for direct employment and people to indirect employment. Fish production in cages become highly popular among the small or limited resources farmers who are looking for alternatives to traditional agricultural crops. This is expected to increase because of the execution of various water projects in the country.

Cage aquaculture through relatively new to the inland aquaculture scenario of the country brings in new opportunities for optimizing fish production from the reservoirs and lakes and also developing new skill among fishers and entrepreneurs to enhance their earning. However unplanned expansion of any activity can lead to adverse impact in terms of environmental integrity and social equity.

INDIAN FISHERY - AN OVERVIEW

In the fishery sector 11847 primary cooperative societies with a total membership of about 13.17 lacks. The total business operation in these societies revolves around Rs 150 Cr. according to the Planning Commission Report 2001.

Table 1.1 Fish production in India and world, 2001- 02 to 20011-12

(in million metric tons)

Year	World	India	India's share %
2001-02	129.00	5.96	4.62
2011-12	150	10.8	7.2

Contribution in Indian Economy

In contribution of fishery sector to the GDP has gone up from 0.46% in 1950- 51, in 1.47 % in 2001-02 and 3.25 % in 2011 - 12. The Agricultural Gross Domestic Product (AgGDP) has impressively increased during this period from 0.84 % to 4.01 %. In fact the fishery sector is booming and contribution increasingly to the economic growth of the nation.

Table 1.2 Contribution and growth of fisheries sector in India

In per cent)

Period	Per cent contribution		Per cent annual growth	
	GDP	**AgGDP**	**Fisheries GDP**	**AgGDP**
1951-52	0.46	0.84	5.63	2.68
2001-02	1.03	4.01	4.71	3.08
2011-12	2.81	5.06	6.30	4.22

Ref: National Account statistics diff vol.

Year	Capture Fish Production		Aquaculture production		Total Fish Production	
	Global	India	Global	India	Global	India
2005	92.0	3.691	99.3	2.967	136.3	6.658(4.88%)
2006	89.7	3.895	97.3	3.180	137.0	7.025(5.13%)
2007	89.9	3.859	99.9	3.112	139.8	6.971(4.99%)
2008	89.7	9.105	52.5	3.979	142.2	7.584(5.33%)
2010	90.0	9.020	55.1	9.27	145.1	8.290(5.71%)

Table 1.3. Share of fisheries in Gross State Domestic Product (GSDP) and in Agricultural State Gross Domestic Product (AgSGDP)

States	Share of fisheries in GSDP			
	1980-81	1990-91	2001-02	2011-12

Table 1.4. Fish production in India and the World and its percent contribution to world fish production.

Sr. no	States	Rivers & canals kms	Reservoirs (Lakh hect.)	Tank & Pond (Lack hect.)
1	Andra Pradesh	11517	2.34	5.17
2	Arunachal Pradesh	2000	-----	2.76
3	Gujarat	3865	2.43	0.71
4	Kerala	3092	0.30	0.30
5	Maharashtra	16000	2.99	0.72

Table1.5 Inland Fishery resources by state and Union Territories.

	SGDP	AgSGDP	SGDP	AgSGDP	SGDP	AgSGDP	SGDP	AgSGDP
Andhra Pradesh	1.2	2.6	0.6	1.7	2.4	7.69	3.1	8.9
Goa	2.3	9.9	2.2	15.18	2.67	23.54	4.12	36.12
West Bengal	3.0	4.4	3.1	9.9	3.14.	11.82	6.7	20.18
Kerala	2.0	5.2	1.8	5.23	1.93	7.81	2.28	9.12
Gujarat	0.8	2.1	1.1	4.3	1.06	6.39	2.19	8.13
Maharashtra	0.6	2.5	0.4	1.7	0.43	2.95	1.28	4.64
Tamilnadu	0.6	2.5	0.3	1.3	0.74	4.38	1.13	6.46

Ref.Fisheries division, D/O Animal Husbandry, Dairying & Fisheries.

Table 1.6. Fish production during 2014-15

(in tone)

Sr. no	State	Marine	Inland	Total
1	Andra Pradesh	475401	1489033	1964434
2	Assam	0	282700	282700
3	Bihar	0	478900	478900
4	Gujarat	698450	111482	809932
5	Kerala	472744	159512	632256
6	Maharashtra	423794	124952	548746
7	Telangana	0	265379	265379
8	West Bengal	178851	1438468	16273 (average)
All India		**3491290**	**6581121**	**10072411**

Ref. Fishery statics : part viii

Table1.7. Fish production in India

(in tones)

Year	Marine	Inland	Total
2000-01	2811	2845	5656
2001-02	2830	3126	5956
2002-03	2990	3210	6200
2003-04	2941	3458	6999
2004-05	2779	3526	6305
2005-06	2816	3756	6572
2006-07	3024	3845	6869
2007-08	2920	4207	7127
2008-09	2978	4639	7617
2009-10	2689	4862	7851
2010-11	3220	5068	8288

Ref: planning commission report 2011

Table.1.8. inland fishery resources in India

Sr.no.	States	Rivers & Canals	Reservoirs	Ponds & Tanks	Beels, oxbow lakes & water bodies	Brackish water
		Km	Million hect.	Million hect.	Million hect.	Million hect.
1	Andhra Pradesh	11514	0.46	0.52	-----	0.06
2	Assam	4820	------	0.02	0.11	----
3	Goa	250	------	Neg.	----	----
4	Gujarat	3865	0.29	0.07	0.01	0.1
5	Himachal Pradesh	3000	0.04	Neg.	----	----
6	Karnataka	9000	0.44	0.44	----	0.1
7	Kerala	3092	0.03	Neg.	0.24	0.24
8	Maharashtra	1600	0.27	0.03	----	-----
9	Rajasthan	5290	0.15	0.18	Neg.	----
10	Andaman & Nicobar	115	-----	0.03	Neg.	----
11	Pondicherry	247	-----	Neg.	Neg.	Neg.

Ref: Handbook on fishery statics ; Report on working group on fisheries for ninth five year plan.

Cage is an enclosed space to rear organism in water that maintains free exchange of water 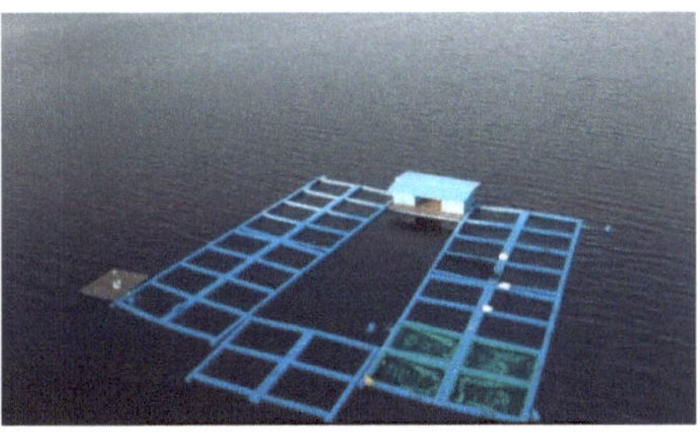 with the surrounding water body. It is an aquaculture production system where fish are held in floating net pens. Cage culture of fish utilizes existing water resources but encloses the fish in a cage or basket which allows water to pass freely between the fish and the pond permitting water exchange and waste removal into the surrounding water

Why cage culture?

The reservoirs of India have a combined surface of area of million hectors, mostly in tropical zone, which makes them the country's most important inland water resources with huge untapped potential, spread across the numerous rivers basin in the country. The success role of auto stocking is very low in Indian reservoirs dry up during the summer, partly or completely with no stock surviving. Stocking with the right fish species, using seeds of appropriate size and producing it at the right time are essential to optimizing fish yield from reservoirs. Though

22 billion fish fry are produced every year in India, there is an acute shortage of fish fingerling available for stocking reservoir. Where fingerlings are available transporting them to Reservoirs usually incur high fingerling mortality. In the context, producing fingerlings in cage offers opportunities for supplying stocking materials, which are vital inputs towards a programme of enhancing fish productions from Indian reservoirs.

ADVANTAGES AND DISADVANTAGES OF CAGE CULTURE

As with any production system, fish culture in cages has advantages and disadvantages that
Should be considered carefully before choosing it as the production model.

Advantages

- Easy Installation.
- Flexibility in management.
- Effective use of fish feeds.
- Less manpower requirement.
- Better control of fish growth.
- In emergencies it can be transfer from one place to another.
- Treatment of disease is much simple than that of pond culture.

- It requires less investment, because use of existing water bodies, and simple technology and swift return of investment.

- Close observation and sampling of fish is simple and therefore only minimum supervision is needed.

- Many types of water resources can be used, including lakes, reservoirs, ponds and rivers.

- Fish handling and harvesting are very simple and helps to maintain the non-seasonal supply of the fish.

- Since the cage is meshed, fish inside have less chances of being attacked by predators.

- They can be used to clean up eutrophicated waters through culture of caged planktivorous species such as silver carp.
- They can be used to clean up eutrophicated waters through culture of caged planktivorous species such as silver carp.

Disadvantages

- Feed must be nutritionally complete and kept fresh.
- Stocked fish simply affected by the external water quality problems e.g. Low oxygen levels.
- Diseases are a common problem in cage culture.
- The crowding in cages promotes stress and allows disease organisms spread rapidly.
- Also, wild fish around the cage can transmit diseases to the caged fish.
- Caged fish are unable to get the natural food of their choice, where as it is readily available to the free fish.
- During feeding a significant amounts of fish feed passes out through the mesh, therefore, fish require feeding many times a day.
- The high fish density with the high feeding rates, often reduce dissolved oxygen and increase ammonia concentration in and around the cage, especially if there is no water movement through the cage.
- In public waters, cage culture faces many competing interests and its legal status is not well defined.

DESIGN AND CONSTRUCTION

Cage range in size from one to several hundred cubic meters and can be any shape but rectangular, square or cylindrical shapes are typical. Cage consists of **Frame**. Cage frame can be constructed from wood, iron, bamboo and HDPE.

FLOATION

Floating cages required a floatation device to stay at the

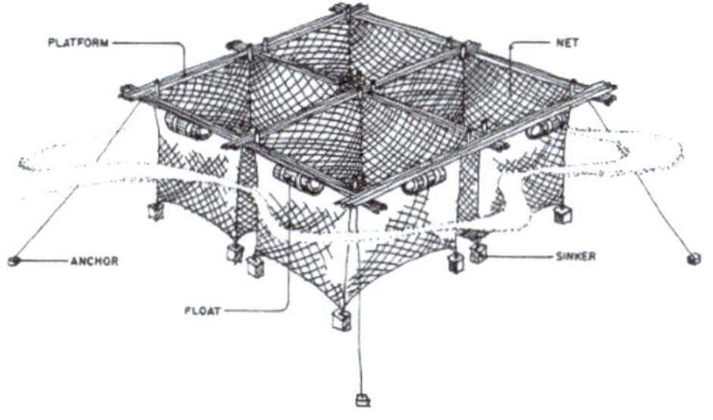

surface. Floating can be provided by metal or plastic drum, sealed PVC pipe or Styrofoam and HDPE pontoon.

MESH OR NETTING : It is made from wire mesh or nylon netting. Plastic netting is durable, rigid, light weight and less expensive than wire mesh.

CAGE COVER : Cage should be equipped with cover to prevent fish loses from jumping or birds predation. Cover are often eliminated on large nylon cages if the top edges of the cage walls are supported 30 to 60 cm above the water surface.

INVIRONMENTAL IMPACT OF CAGE CULTURE

1. The surface of cage culture depends on maintaining good water quality around the fish cages.

2. Nutrient enrichment of water that many lead to increase algae growth.

3. The environmental impact of cage culture can be minimised through proper site selection and keeping food wastage in low level and higher food conversion ratio.

WATER QUALITY

1. DISSOLVED OXYGEN (DO)

Dissolved oxygen level and its availability are critical to the health and survival of caged fish. It must be 4 mg per litre.

2. TEMPRETURE

The most important physical factor controlling the life of a cold blooded animal like fish is temperature. Each species of fish has an optimum temperature range for growth as well as upper and lower lethal temperature.

3. pH

Uptake and released of CO2 during photosynthesis and respiration affect Ph in a cage and due to this, it fluctuate daily. The desirable range of early morning Ph for fish production is from 6.5 to 9.

<u>STEPS OF CAGE CULTURE</u>

1. TYPE OF CAGES

Four types of cages are used in cage aquaculture fixed, floating, submersible and submerged.

The fix cage is the most basic and wildly used in shallow water with a depth of 1 to 3 meters. It consist of net bag fitted to post and is normally placed in the flow in the streets cannons, rivers and reservoirs. Fixed cages are comparatively expensive and simple but there use is restricted. Floating cage on the other hand supported by a floating frame such that the net bag hangs in water without touching the bottom. Floating cages are generally used in water bodies with a depth of more than five meter. Enormous diversity in size, shape and design has been developed for floating cages to suit the wild range of condition of fish culture in water. The net bags of submersible cages are suspended from the surface have adjustable buoyancy and may be registered or flexible. Submerged net bag are filled in a solid and rugged frame and submerged under the water.

2. SITE SELECTION

Site selection is the most important part of the cage culture. Proper selection of a site reduce must of the problem arise with cage culture and operational cost. The cage units should built to withstand preventing wind and wave condition at the selected site. Good water exchange is also important in cage culture to replenish oxygen and flush away wastage.

Before attempting cage culture in and existing water body, the following criteria should be considered.

1. At least 5 meter should separate each cage to optimise water quality.

2. Water quality and circulation should be good from local and industrial pollution.

3. The water level not fluctuate greatly (0.5 to 1.0 m)

4. They should be safe from frequent disturbance from local people and animals.

5. There should be accessed to land and water transportation.

6. Site should be secure.

PROCUREMENT OF CAGE MATERIALS

Making cage culture economically viable demand the preparation of a comprehensive just of material available any local market.

1. PONTOONS

Pontoons (also called **Floats**) are airtight hollow structures, similar to pressure vessels, designed to provide buoyancy in water. Flotation can be provided by metal or plastic drums, sealed PVC pipe, or Styrofoam. Cages require this flotation (**Pontoons**) device to stay at the surface. Their principal applications are in **pontoon bridge construction**. Floats should be placed around the cage so that it floats evenly with the lid about 30 cm out of the water.

2. SINKERS

Sinkers are local available stones, weighing 3 to 4 kg that is triggered to the Bamboo frame with nylon rope. At the corners and long the side to help cages maintain their rectangular shape. The bottom portion of netlon cages is tied to the nylon rope running down to the sinker but the rope maintains the shape of the cage. Eight netlon required 48 sinkers, with 8 sinkers maintaining the underwater shape of each cage.

3. ANCHORS

Lange conceit stone weighting 40 to 50 kg or more are used Anchors that rest on the reservoirs bottom to hold the cages in place. Two anchors are tied with Garware brand thick nylon rope to every corner of the frame and another anchor is tied to the centre of each long side, thus requiring 10 stone for each cage.

3. NETLON

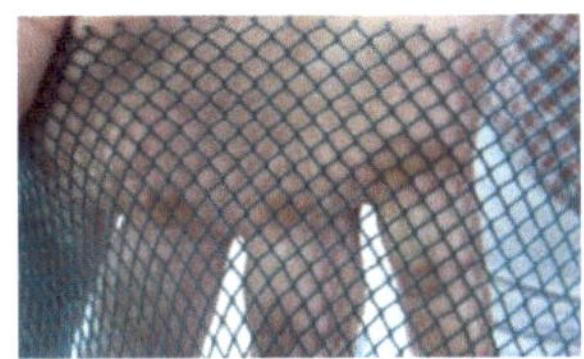

High density propylene extract (HDPE) plasto-nets with 1.5 mm mesh are used to prepare netlon cages for rearing fingerlings to > 100 mm from fry initially measuring 10 to 25 mm. A rectangular cages measuring 6×4×4 cubic meter is convenient to operate. The cage is totally enclosed with netlon on all four sides, the bottom and the top (to prevent predations by birds). Small flap opening at top corners allow feeding and harvesting. The netlon

should be well stitched with doubly lived nylon ribbon 3.8 cm in width at the corners and joint with loops at the corners and sides. The some nylon ribbon stitches tighter the upper and lower lids at regular intervals to make the cage sturdier. The cages are hung from pontoons frame and tied with the sinkers at the bottom corners to keep them straight and hanging vertical. Thus the battery of 12 net has a good functional volume of 360 cubic meter of which 320 cubic meters (96 cubic meters in each cage) is under water.

The net cages are tied with silk rope to the frame to keep them straight. Wants the frame is anchored at the culture side, the next step is to tie on the netlon cages, twelve to a battery. Along the top, silk ropes are used to tie the net to the bamboo frame firmly to prevent sagging; sinkers are tight to the bottom corners and side of the netlon cages to hold them vertical. The hanging net cages should remain at least 1.2 meter above the lake bottom to avoid damage cause by crabs and other bottom dwellers. Local fisher should be instructed not to tie there gillnets to the frame as this may damage it. The net cages should be left in the water for at least a week before stocking to allow algae on grow on the netting. Curing the net thus reduces injury to fry.

INSTALLIONS OF CAGES

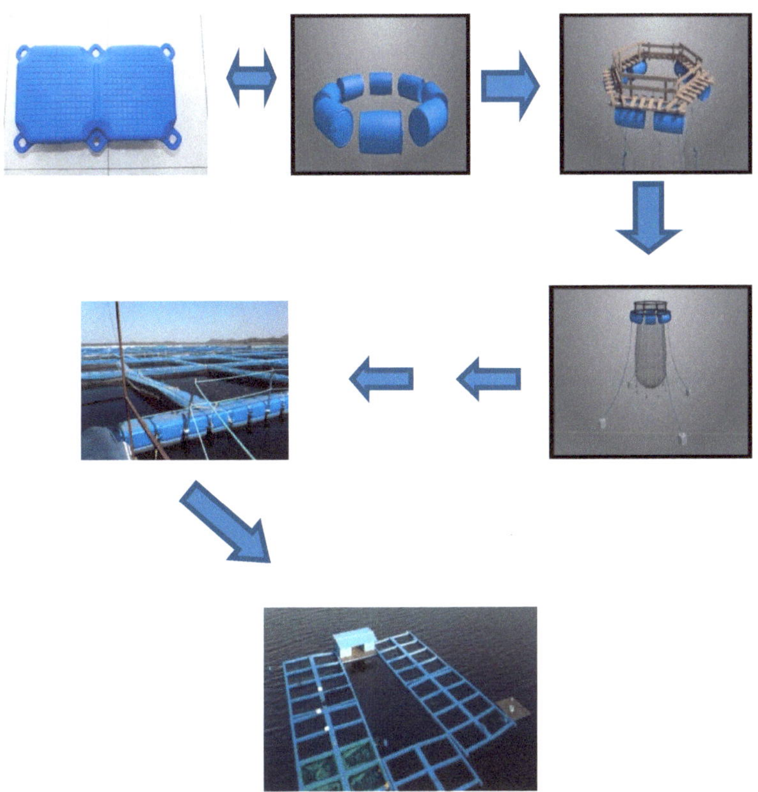

SELLECTION OF STOCKING MATERIALS

Many species are suitable to grow in cages. The present objective is produce fingerling primarily of Indian Major Carp

as well as to grow same common carp (*Cyprinus carpio*) and grass carp (ctenophyryngodon idella) provided that the food inches are sufficient  for their further growth after stocking in the reservoirs. First the locality should be surveyed to see what stocking species are available. Pangasius are easily available in West Bengal, Gujrat and Hydrabad. Fry must be transported from West Bengal, where carps are available and less expensive than in other part of India. If transported packed with oxygen, the fry can withstand a journey of 40 hours, the fry should be healthy perched and come from deem water body with low eutrophication. For raising fingerlings in cages in Indian reservoirs, healthy carp fry measuring 12 to 15 mm long, or even up to 25 mm are best suited. Advanced fry longer than 35 mm should be avoided for cage culture to fingerlings size, as they routinely are affected by fungal diseases.

such as Seprolegniosis if collected if collected from nurseries that have atrophied. At the moment economically viable cage culture is practiced in inland water bodies of India by growing the Pangasius (sutchi catfish) Pangasiunodon hypophthalmus, fry should be shifted late in the day or early in the evening to allowing conditioning at the site of procurement and acclimatization at the site of release in cage. Conditioning is required to transport the fry with empty stomach, as the ammonia and carbon dioxide generated by fish waste may prove lethal to fry during transport. Fry acclimatization is essential at the site of release in cages to ensure a balanced environment, especially in terms of temperature. The oxygen packets transported with the fry (1000 fry in 4 litters of water in polythene packets 2/3 filled with oxygen) are kept inside cages for at least a hour before the fry are released. Prior to release, fry are subjected to some prophylactic measures to protect them from diseases and ecoto-parasites. They are dipped in the 5 to 6 per cent salt solutions as well as potassium permanganate (5 to 8%) for 1 to 2 minutes and they realised into the cage water.

PANGASIUS

Pangasius cat fish exhibited excellent growth and feed conversion efficiency with soya meal based fry, fingerling and grow out feeds pangasius growth was rapid, with fish growing from 0.1 gm to 880 gm in 181 days. Conforming ability to produces market size fish from imported fry within the single growing season. Pangasius growth during stage to exceed the target

production size of 600 gm by 47% in 78 days pangasius were aggressive freedom with the soya based feeds. No diseases problems were encountered during the trial. No drugs or chemical were used, providing a healthy "green" market product. Pangasius is having a streamlined body, dark grey coloured back, silver belly wide mouth and long twin beard, Pangasius has more red blood cells than other fishes, an additional respiratory organ and can breathe through hobbles and skin. This means it has able to tolerate environments with little dissolved oxygen. Its growth rate is rapidly and it can live in the wide far as long as 20 years. After around 2 month during breeding it reaches about 10 to 12 cm long and 14 to 15 gm in weights while the age of 10, it can reach around 25 kg in farming pond and weighting between 800 to 1100 gm in 6 to 8 months are best for harvesting. The culture of Pangasius primarily reared in pond and cages, pangasius is usually stocked at high densities (around 60 to 80 fish per square metre) and grown for around 6 to 8 month before reaching its harvest weight of around 1kg.

MAINTAINCE

1. CAGE MAINTAINCE

Cage should be deemed at 15 days interval to avoid net clogging. After shifting the stock to another cage, each cage is taken out, sun dried and cleaned thoroughly by scrubbing or water get wash to remove debris and fowling organisms. The physicochemical parameters of water should be recorded regularly as a part of water quality monitoring.

2. MONOTORING WATER QUALITY

Water quality parameter must be monitored in the cages are dissolved oxygen, acidity, free ammonia and phosphate, Indian reservoirs normally maintain water parameters suitable for rearing fingerlings in cages, though very rarely an algal bloom may push some parameters to the point of treating fish survival.

3. CLEANING NETLON CAGES

Cages should be cleaned with soft brush fortnightly to remove algae, sponges and other organism. Floating microphysics that waves sometimes push against cages should also be removed; any dead fish should be removed from cages immediately and disposed of in a pit. Covering dead fish with line helps contain any disease.

ROUTINE CHECKING

Loose twine, mesh torn by predators, anchors and sinkers must be checked routinely and immediately mended or replaced as needed. Repair torm mesh with patches to keep fry from escaping. With the outset of bad weather, anchors should be checked and fastened tightly.

4. FISH STOCK MONOTORING

Routine checks of fish health help prevent massive fry loss. Fish health can be easily checked monitoring fry response when feed is applied. Signs of ill health include surfacing, lesions, rashes, spots, lumps; excessive mucus formations woolly mat formation, bulging eyes and fin and tail erosions. Appropriate prophylactic measures should be applied as necessary and at least fortnightly. Remove the fry from the cages and soak them or 2 minutes 5 to 6 % salt solution followed by 5 to 8% potassium permanganate solution to eradicate ecoto-parasites. A 20 to 30 % potassium permanganate solution may be spread on the water surface inside the cages. At time, a time solution may be spread inside the cages to clean the water.

5. MONOTORING OF GROWTH RATE

Samples should be taken at a regular interval to asses fry length and weight to monitor growth. This information is important for maintaining fish health and optimal feeding, as well as scheduling the harvest.

SUPPLIMENTARY FEEDING

Feeding is essential for fry in captivity, as the natural food in many Indian reservoirs may not be sufficient for their growth even to fingerlings size, feeds should be available locally and expensive to contain production cost. Carp except a wide varieties of feed, providing a range of option for selecting locally available feed ingredient with an eye on cost. In general rice brain and mustard oil cake blended 1:1 provide a mixture with vitamins amino acid and minerals available at concentration of 0.01%.

As the cages installed in reservoirs and subjected to waves it's not advisable to provide supplementary feed in floating trays, as is the practise in cage installed in wet lands or calm legs, in general the fine, flaky powdered form of rice brain and mustard oil cake mixed together is spreading over the water surface inside each cage twice daily at 8:00 and 17:00 hours at a rate of 3 to 5% of aggregate fry body weight initially 3 to 4 kgs of feed are applied per cages per day.

FEED REQUIREMENT OF PANGASIANODON HYPOPHTHALUS IN CAGE CULTURE

Average body weight (gm)	Average feed(gm.)	No. of feeding/day
0>50	3.3	2-3
50>100	4.8	2-3
100>250	5.8	2-3
250>500	8.4	2-3
500>750	9.4	1-2
750>1000	10.5	1-2
1000>1500	11.0	1-2
>1500	12.0	1-2

Average body weight (g)	Feeding %	No. of feeding/day	Name of the feed
0-10	4-5	2-3	Rice bran
10-25	3-4	2-3	Spoiled & discarded cooking eggs
>30	3-4	Once in 3 days	Chicken waste raw & boiled

MARKET ANALYSIS

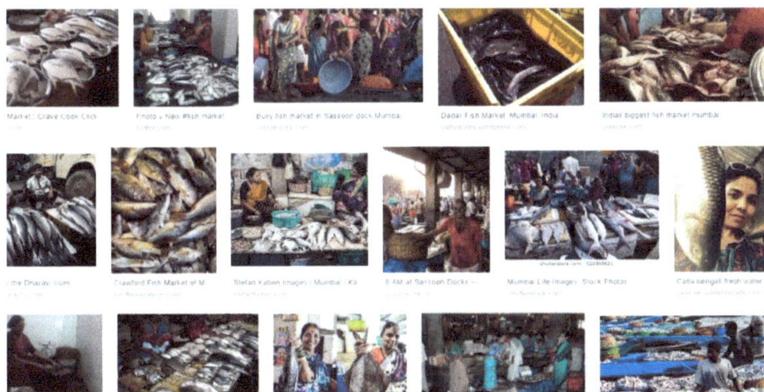

Retailers buy fish from Wholesaling center of higher secondary or secondary markets. They sell fish directly to the consumers either through fixed stall or by vending from head/rickshaws. From the start of the distribution channel, fish at the secondary market to city or terminal markets. Intermediaries operating on different level performing marketing function like cleaning, sorting, boxing, icing, repacking and arranging for transportation etc. At each market level wholesalers and retailers may be supplying fish to local consumers.

Marketing channels for open water fish catches

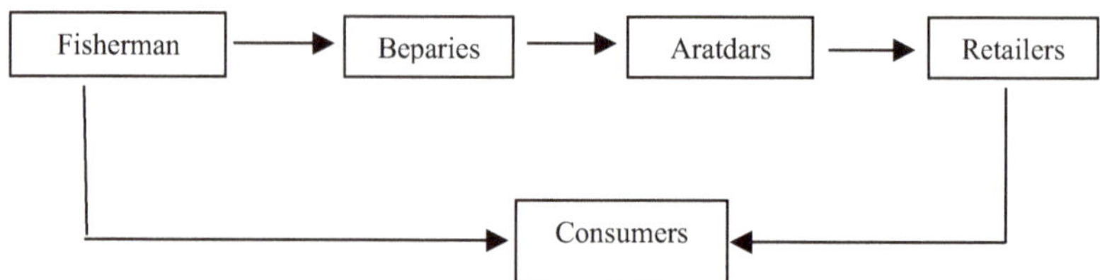

Marketing channels for Cage culture

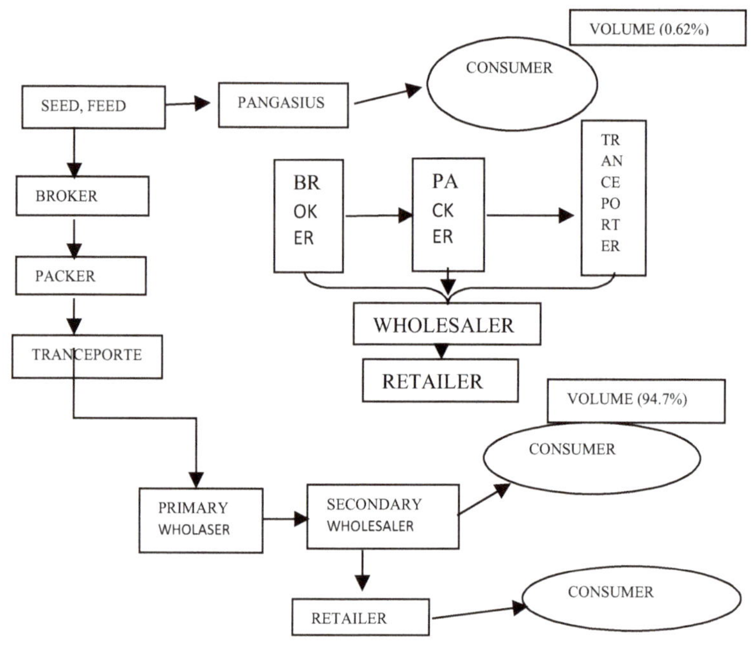

DEMAND

India is famous for freshwater Fish. Mostly people like to eat Indian major carp, common carp, Prawns, Pegasus and Tilapia. Maharashtra in India is having big market for fish. Mostly transport fish to , China, Australia, Japan and South Africa. Mumbai is the big market for Pangasius fish.

Mostly we transported fish to Hyderabad, Kolkata, Gujarat and Bihar.

YELDARI DAM
(General Information)

Yeldari Dam, is an earth fill dam on Prune river near Yeldari in Jintur taluka of Parbhani district in the state of Maharashtra in India. It is the second largest dam in Marathwada region. Dam is renovated and developed as a big reservoir and also tourist attraction spot and fresh water fishery in Parbhani district. The height of the dam above its lowest foundation is 51.2 m (168 ft) while the length is 4,232 m (13,885 ft). The live storage capacity is 0.81 km^3 (0.19 cu mi). The dam was built between 1958 and 1968. It has a hydroelectric power station consisting of three units of 7.5 MW. Capacity each for 22.5 MW total capacities.

LUMBINI
BLUE REVOLUTION OF INDIA

Plant Visit

42

THANK YOU